IMAGES
of America

THE PORT OF LONG BEACH

ON THE COVER: The year was 1916 and the Port of Long Beach was just five years old when this Hammond Lumber Company steam schooner unloaded her cargo of cut redwood at the port's new Municipal Pier. Over the following 90-plus years, millions of containers and countless tons of cargo from oil and automobiles to cement and oranges have passed through the port's cargo-handling facilities. (Courtesy of the Port of Long Beach Archive.)

IMAGES
of America

THE PORT OF LONG BEACH

Michael D. White

ARCADIA
PUBLISHING

ISBN 978-0-7385-6985-7

Published by Arcadia Publishing
Charleston, South Carolina

Printed in the United States of America

Library of Congress Control Number: 2008934516

For all general information contact Arcadia Publishing at:
Telephone 843-853-2070
Fax 843-853-0044
E-mail sales@arcadiapublishing.com
For customer service and orders:
Toll-Free 1-888-313-2665

Visit us on the Internet at www.arcadiapublishing.com

Dedicated to Elmar Baxter.

Contents

ACKNOWLEDGMENTS

My sincere gratitude goes to Art Wong, assistant director of communications and senior media relations officer for the Port of Long Beach, and Kirsten Parker, supervisor of the port's Record Center, for their kindness in granting me access to the extensive archive of images and materials compiled by the port over the past 100 years.

Sincere thanks for their patient assistance in helping with the research for this book also go out to the reference staffs of the Long Beach Public Library, the Burbank Public Library, the Glendale Public Library, the Pasadena Public Library, and the staff of the Graphics Department at Azusa Pacific University.

Paula Korn, public relations manager of SeaLaunch LLC; Ron Alger of the Long Beach Fire Department Museum; and the Public Relations offices of both the U.S. Navy and U.S. Coast Guard are also due my appreciation, as are those of the Cunard Steamship Company, the Pacific Harbor Line, the Matson Navigation Company, the R.M.S. *Queen Mary*, photographer Andy Witherspoon, and the Connolly-Pacific Corporation.

My heartfelt thanks also go to Jerry Roberts and Devon Weston of Arcadia Publishing and my family, particularly my wife, Pam, for their support, patience, and understanding.

INTRODUCTION

In January 1853, Capt. John Rodgers, U.S. Navy, was allocated a budget of $125,000 and commissioned by a farseeing Congress to "prosecute a survey and reconnaissance for naval and commercial purposes, of such parts of the Bering Straits, of the North Pacific Ocean and of the China Seas, as are frequented by American whale ships and by trading vessels in their routes between the United States and China."

His mission accomplished three years later, Rodgers summarized his experience in a letter to the Secretary of the Navy, which he closed with a remarkable prescient observation. He wrote: "We, through California, inherit the trade of the Pacific; for we are the only nation upon it which cultivates foreign commerce . . . my sense of its importance [that is, the just completed survey] has been quickened by seeing the wonderful energy of California, and her progress under its influence."

A little more than 50 years later, celebrating the arrival of one of the first ships to call at the port's new one-and-only pier in the summer of 1911, the *Long Beach Daily Telegram* opined that the event marked "an important epoch, it being the forerunner of a large commerce which is destined to come into the local harbor."

That "local harbor" was the Port of Long Beach. Neither Rodgers nor the unnamed *Daily Telegram* editorialist could ever have fantasized that a few years later one of the most productive, and unlikely, of those inheritors would be ranked among the busiest and most advanced deepwater ports in the world.

Imagined into existence on 800 acres of tidal wetlands, over the past century the port has blossomed from a single 500-foot wooden pier to a giant complex sprawled across 3,200 acres with on-dock rail capability at 10 of its piers, accommodating 80 deepwater berths served by 71 of the most modern container cranes in existence.

Currently weighing in as the second busiest port in the United States, the Port of Long Beach would, if combined with its neighboring Port of Los Angeles, be the fifth most active port complex in the entire world.

An average of 5,300 ships currently call at the port every year with the staggering total of 7.3 million containers moving through its facilities in 2007, a volume accounting for a full 33 percent of all the containers moving through all California ports, more than a quarter of the total number of containers handled by all North American West Coast ports, and 13 percent of the total crossing the docks of all U.S. ports.

In 2008, the Port of Long Beach was named the best seaport in North America by the Singapore-based industry newspaper *Cargonews Asia*. It was the fourth consecutive year and the 12th time in the past 13 years that the port has been recognized as the best on the continent, despite strong competition from such giants as Seattle, Oakland, the Port of New York/New Jersey, and the neighboring Port of Los Angeles.

It would be the epitome of understatement to say that the port has come a long way since the first cargoes of redwood lumber crossed its first municipal pier almost 100 years ago.

A long way for certain through a channel dredged, almost literally, by stalwart boosters like Long Beach mayors Charles Windham, W. T. Lisenby, and C. A. Buffum; banker P. E. Hatch; shipbuilder James F. Craig; chamber of commerce president Charles van de Water; California state senator Frank Flint; and countless, anonymous laborers, mariners, engineers, and staffers like harbormaster C. F. White led by the likes of hard-driving harbor superintendents and general managers like R. G. McGlone, Eloi Amar, Charles Vickers, Thomas Thorley, James McJunkin, Steven Dillenbeck, and, most recently, Richard Steinke.

Also on the list of those who have labored so tirelessly on the port's behalf over the years is Elmar Baxter, who served as director of Public Relations from 1970 to 1990.

A Southern California native and accomplished newspaper editor and writer, Baxter graduated from the U.S. Merchant Marine Academy and served as an officer on Liberty ships during World War II. During two decades of its most significant development, Baxter helped successfully position the port as it grew in both size and influence and, among many other accomplishments, was the primary driving force in creating OPSail '84, the visit of a fleet of tall ships that called at the port during the 1984 Los Angeles Olympics.

Following his retirement from the port in 1990, Elmar Baxter was largely responsible for starting the challenging work of archiving the port's huge collection of images, which comprise such a large part of this book. He died on December 29, 2007, while this work was being researched and written.

As he was dedicated to the Port of Long Beach, this book is dedicated to him.

One

"A Truly Fine Site"

Through the late 1880s and the 1890s, the newly minted City of Long Beach cast an eager eye toward the bitter struggle raging between neighboring San Pedro and distant Santa Monica for the government's blessing to be developed into Southern California's deepwater port.

The battle was decided in 1897 in San Pedro's favor. Long Beach initially sought merely an adjunct role in San Pedro's development, serving as a residential community for workers building the new harbor.

Over time, the energy channeled into developing neighboring San Pedro and Wilmington diminished as Long Beach visionaries touted a port for their city. "It may yet develop that one need not go to Wilmington to secure a truly fine site on the great Inner Harbor," editorialized the *Long Beach Press* on July 21, 1903.

Ensuing years saw almost ceaseless channel dredging and the steady development of the harbor by hundreds of workers. Improved rail access and pier construction were top priorities. Industries came, led by the Craig Shipbuilding Company, which relocated from Toledo, Ohio, in 1907. Four years later, Craig launched the 266-foot steamer *General Hubbard*, the first steel ship ever built in Southern California. Also relocating to Long Beach were the American Potash Company, Coronado Chemical Company, Long Beach Iron Works, Sea Salt Soap Company, Star Drilling Machine Company, and the improbably named Looff Amusement Device Company.

The first merchant ships called at the new Port of Long Beach in 1911, the steam schooners *Casco* in May and the *Iaqua* in June. They unloaded lumber cargoes, marking the first use of Pier 1 Municipal Dock, the port's first deepwater wharf. On June 24, the Port of Long Beach was officially dedicated with the visit of the lumber steamer *Santa Barbara*. Growth followed rapidly. In February 1912, the steamer *Northland* became the first ship to board passengers "for distant points"—San Francisco and Seattle—while in April 1914 alone, more than 30 lumber ships called at the Municipal Dock, discharging more than two million board feet of lumber.

The World War I years saw shipbuilding advance as a major industry at the port with a score of Emergency Fleet freighters, five submarines, and a lighthouse tender at yards operated jointly by Craig and Long Beach Shipbuilding Company. The stage was set for the Port of Long Beach to slide into a future of unprecedented growth on skids liberally lubricated with black gold.

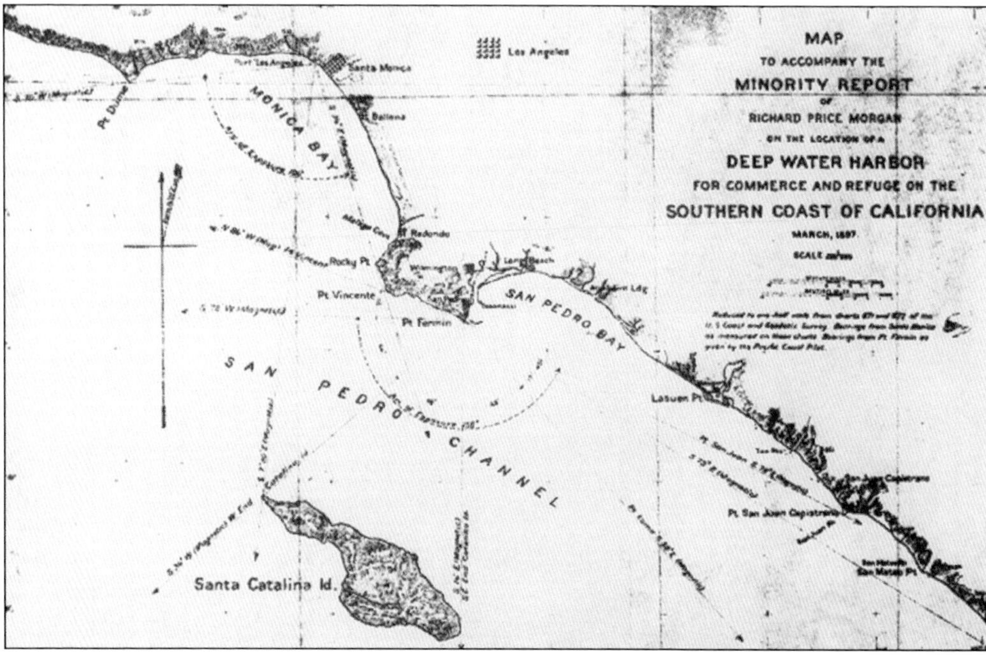

PROPOSED PORTS, 1897. This chart of San Pedro Bay was an exhibit for the U.S. Senate hearings held in Washington, D.C., to study recommendations for the proposed sites of the ports of Los Angeles and, later, Long Beach. (Courtesy of the Port of Long Beach Archive.)

DOWNTOWN LONG BEACH, 1899. A busy Saturday afternoon is pictured here, looking north from the corner of First Street and Pine Avenue. From 1890 to 1910, the city's population skyrocketed from 564 people to more than 17,800, largely due to the steady development of the port. (Courtesy of the Port of Long Beach Archive.)

Craig Shipbuilding Company, 1906. Construction starts at the future home of the 40-acre ship construction and repair yard, which would become the only ship construction and repair facility on the U.S. West Coast south of San Francisco. (Courtesy of the Port of Long Beach Archive.)

Dredging Plans, 1906. Work began on a plan to dredge three channels and a 1,400-foot turning basin that would create an Inner Harbor with more than 25,000 feet of frontage with five berths and warehouse space on the 800 acres of tidal flats west of the city of Long Beach. (Courtesy of the Port of Long Beach Archive.)

VISIONARY MAYOR, 1908. Charles H. Windham was one of the earliest, and most active, proponents of developing the new port. According to his official biography, Windham was born in Tennessee in 1871 and began his career working as a blacksmith's helper and bridge carpenter's assistant on the old California and Oregon Railroad. Over the next several years, Windham worked on several railroads in many different capacities, eventually buying a coffee and sugar plantation in Costa Rica before moving his family to Long Beach. Over a 20-year period, he served not only as mayor for two terms, from 1908 to 1912, but also as city manager and postmaster. He was responsible for overseeing the development of the Long Beach portion of the San Pedro Bay breakwater, and his vigorous support for the harbor during its formative years led many to consider him the "Father of Long Beach Harbor." Windham died in Florida on April 11, 1932. (Courtesy of the author's collection.)

TERMINAL ISLAND LINK, 1908. The Salt Lake Railway connected Long Beach to Terminal Island with a single track over a wooden trestle. The trestle blocked deepwater access to the Craig shipyard and was replaced with a 187-foot bascule drawbridge, one of the largest bridges of its kind in the country. (Courtesy of the Port of Long Beach Archive.)

BUILDING AND REPAIR, 1909. Five unidentified schooners nested at the Craig shipyard await repairs and refitting. The yard was the first major industry to establish itself in the harbor, a full three years before the port was officially dedicated. (Courtesy of the Port of Long Beach Archive.)

Open to the Ocean, 1909. A dredge operated by the Los Angeles Dock and Terminal Company cuts through the last of three sandbars to open the Inner Harbor to the ocean. Completion of the dredging project marked a major milestone in the ability of the port to handle deepwater ships. (Courtesy of the Port of Long Beach Archive.)

The Port Opens for Business, 1909. August 28, 1909, marked the official opening of the Port of Long Beach as the last sediment was dredged from the opening of the harbor's Main Channel. The electric dredge used for the work was built at the nearby Craig shipyard. (Courtesy of the Port of Long Beach Archive.)

FIRST LAUNCH, 1910. Dignitaries, including Long Beach mayor Charles H. Windham (front row with hat in hand), gathered to celebrate the launch of the 266-foot *General Hubbard*, the first steel steamship built in Southern California. The ship was built by the Craig Shipbuilding Company, formerly of Toledo, Ohio, for the Hammond Lumber Company and was the first to sail through the recently dredged entrance to the port's Inner Harbor. Able to carry 1.5 million metric feet of cut lumber, the *General Hubbard* was built at a cost of $266,000 and was powered by a pair of 1,500-horsepower, triple-expansion steam engines, which were also built at the yard's machine shop. A crowd of more than 10,000 people gathered to watch Ruth Craig, daughter of shipyard owner James F. Craig, christen the ship. (Courtesy of the Port of Long Beach Archive.)

PIER D, 1910. A single rail track rides the ridge of the dike that forms the foundation of Pier D. Until the Inner Harbor was opened to deepwater ships, Pier D was the port's only wharf capable of docking visiting large steamships and sailing vessels. (Courtesy of the Port of Long Beach Archive.)

OPEN FOR BUSINESS, 1911. May 24 marked the official opening of the Port of Long Beach. Citizens attending the event watch Mayor Charles H. Windham celebrate the event by being lifted aboard the steam schooner SS *Casco*, the first ship to unload a cargo—275,000 feet of redwood lumber—at the new Port of Long Beach. (Courtesy of the Port of Long Beach Archive.)

First Pier Lumber Shipment, 1911. The lumber carrier SS *Iaqua* (seen above some years after the event) called at the Port of Long Beach on June 2 with a cargo of 280,000 feet of redwood lumber from Eureka. The lumber was the first cargo to be handled at the port's new 500-foot Municipal Pier. (Courtesy of the Port of Long Beach Archive.)

Floating Drydock, 1911. In September, the three-masted lumber schooner *Lucy* was the first ship to be overhauled in the Craig shipyard's new 204-foot-long, 100-foot-wide floating drydock. The structure utilized seven pontoons and was the first floating drydock to go into service in Southern California. It remained in use until 1970. (Courtesy of the author's collection.)

New Coastal Service, 1912. The North Pacific Steamship Company inaugurated a new weekly express cargo and passenger route with the liner *Santa Clara*, linking Long Beach with San Francisco via Santa Barbara. Despite the fact that the line had been offered free dockage at the port, an unfortunate lack of business ended the much-heralded service after just a few weeks. (Courtesy of the Port of Long Beach Archive.)

Silent Service, 1919. Launched in 1912, the submarine USS *F-2* spent her entire career in the Pacific Fleet as a part of the Submarine Force, U.S. Pacific Fleet. She can be seen above undergoing repairs in dry dock at the Long Beach Navy Yard just a few months after the end of World War I. (Courtesy of the U.S. Navy Historical Center.)

Two

Black Gold and Dark Clouds

Despite political infighting and the obstacles thrown up by several antigrowth groups, the postwar years saw continued development of the port's facilities and a general growth pattern that was to continue through the boom years of the 1920s and the Great Depression right up to the months preceding America's entry into World War II.

The petroleum industry became a major driver in the development of the port when oil was discovered in the neighboring community of Signal Hill in 1921. By the end of the following year, almost 19 million barrels of crude were pumped out of the ground. Two years later, oil production had almost quadrupled to 69 million barrels.

Fifteen years later, oil would be found on port property. In 1938, the first well was drilled, providing revenues to both the port and the city and, unintentionally, setting the stage for chronic subsidence problems that would plague the port over the next three decades.

In 1925, Congress passed the Harbors and Rivers Appropriation Bill, which authorized $3.5 million for the continuing Outer Harbor development at the Port of Long Beach and, over the next several years, bond issues raised almost $8 million for the further development of additional piers, wharves, and terminal facilities. Three years later, the work was completed on the harbor breakwater and east and west moles and bulkheads to protect the harbor entrance.

The unprecedented growth of Southern California in the years between the two world wars more than validated the need for two San Pedro Bay deepwater ports. The port handled 1.1 million tons of cargo in 1926 and, just four years later, the port saw its cargo volume surged fourfold to 4.5 million tons.

Industrialist Henry Ford decided to build an auto assembly plant at the port in July 1930, while, just a few months later, Proctor and Gamble saw that a factory at a major deepwater port like Long Beach would give it access to the rich markets of the Far East.

By 1937, 20 million tons of import and import cargo moved across the port's docks.

As war clouds gathered to the east and the west, the Port of Long Beach would soon find itself catapulted into a critical defense role perfectly positioned for growth in the postwar years.

Last Days of Sail, 1920. An unidentified three-masted ship enters the Port of Long Beach. In the ensuing years, the number of cargo-carrying sailing vessels calling at the port shrank and the last of the once-proud square-riggers seen at the port were burned to the waterline for their metal or converted into fuel or sand barges. (Courtesy of the Port of Long Beach Archive.)

Aerial, 1921. A bird's-eye view of the port shows significant development and a variety of ships from the U.S. Pacific Fleet anchored in the distance. The port was an important base for the navy, which, 10 years later, would make it the home port for a number of capital and auxiliary ships. (Courtesy of the Port of Long Beach Archive.)

Cerritos Channel, 1922. Originally a knee-deep slough separating Terminal Island from the "mainland," the waterway was eventually deepened to a depth of 20 feet and widened to 200 feet. The channel still serves as the primary link between the Port of Long Beach and the neighboring Port of Los Angeles. (Courtesy of the Port of Long Beach Archive.)

Historic First Call, 1924. The Japanese freighter *Chichubu Maru* was the first fully refrigerated ship to visit the Port of Long Beach. The ship was part of the Nippon Yusen Kaisha (NYK) fleet and made regular calls at both Long Beach and San Diego. (Courtesy of the Port of Long Beach Archive.)

Rock Quarry, 1925. A significant amount of the millions of tons of rock used to build the San Pedro Bay breakwater and the moles and bulkheads constructed to protect the harbor from tidal damage were quarried at a huge quarry near Riverside, about 80 miles east of the port. The rock was hauled to the port by the Union Pacific Railroad and then by barge to work sites around the harbor. (Courtesy of the Port of Long Beach Archive.)

Breakwater Construction, 1925. Rock for the breakwater splashes into San Pedro Bay. The breakwater, one of the longest ever built in the United States, eventually stretched 8.4 miles across the bay, providing both the ports of Long Beach and Los Angeles with protection from heavy weather and erosion to the present day. (Courtesy of the Port of Long Beach Archive.)

THE MAN IN CHARGE, 1925. Capt. Cody Markley, field superintendent for the Long Beach portion of the breakwater, strikes a pose next to one of the steam shovels used on the project. Markley was a highly regarded expert in hydrology and had served during World War I as an officer in the U.S. Army Corps of Engineers. (Courtesy of the Port of Long Beach Archive.)

LOCAL BUS SERVICE, 1925. A clutch of schooners, a tanker, and several pleasure craft provide a background for a bus operated by the B&H Transportation Company. The bus operated on the route between the port and Anaheim Street in downtown Long Beach. (Courtesy of the Port of Long Beach Archive.)

PIER A, 1926. Long Beach mayor Ray R. Clark (center) officiated at the official start of construction on Pier A in the port's Outer Harbor. The port was finally thrown open to deep-draft ships in July and handled a total of 1.1 million tons of cargo valued at almost $12 million during the year, up from 358,899 tons in 1925. (Courtesy of the Port of Long Beach Archive.)

CIVIC PRIDE, 1926. A meeting of civic leaders, businessmen, and other interested citizens attended an outdoor lunch at the port to discuss plans to organize the Pacific Southwest Exposition. Two years later, their efforts to promote the city and the port paid off handsomely with the event drawing more than one million visitors. (Courtesy of the Port of Long Beach Archive.)

INNER HARBOR, 1927. Pictured is a view of the Inner Harbor with the Cerritos Channel winding into the distance toward the neighboring Port of Los Angeles. The Graham Brothers rock yard is at left center, while a tanker loads its cargo at the Richfield Oil Company terminal in the foreground. (Courtesy of the Port of Long Beach Archive.)

UNIDENTIFIED WORKERS, 1927. Despite the use of sophisticated dredges and a variety of other modern equipment, much of the work to develop the Port of Long Beach in its earliest days was done by scores of nameless manual laborers like these, who used more basic tools to accomplish their tasks. (Courtesy of the Port of Long Beach Archive.)

Rio Grande Dock, 1927. The tanker *Torres* and a fuel barge are tied up to the dock as a pair of sailing ships nest in the background awaiting their ultimate fate. Within a few months, construction would begin on Piers A and B in the port's Outer Harbor and Pier 1 would be rebuilt as the Municipal Wharf. (Courtesy of the Port of Long Beach Archive.)

Richfield Oil, 1927. Another aerial view of Channel 3 in the port's Inner Harbor shows an unidentified tanker berthed at the Richfield Oil Company terminal. To the left is the Graham Brothers facility that processed a substantial amount of the rock used in construction projects at the port. (Courtesy of the Port of Long Beach Archive.)

Rock Work, 1927. The tedious work of dumping load after load of rock continued on the San Pedro Bay breakwater and the two east and west moles and bulkheads to protect the harbor entrance. The tedious, four-year project was finally completed in 1928. (Courtesy of the Port of Long Beach Archive.)

British Visitor, 1928. The freighter *City of Glasgow* called at the port to load bunker fuel on her way south from British Columbia before transiting the Panama Canal on her return voyage to Northern Europe. The ship was operated by the Ellerman Line. (Courtesy of the Port of Long Beach Archive.)

Bulkhead Construction, 1928. With the end of the project in sight, a barge-mounted crane dumps more rock from the Riverside quarry into the framework of a bulkhead being built to protect the harbor mouth from tidal erosion. (Courtesy of the Port of Long Beach Archive.)

Inner Harbor, 1928. Another perspective of the port's Inner Harbor shows a freighter, riding high in the water, waiting to load a cargo of cotton and dwarfing several lumber schooners berthed nearby. In the distance sprawled the growing city of Long Beach, which already boasted several modest skyscrapers. (Courtesy of the Port of Long Beach Archive.)

TANKER TRAFFIC, 1928. An unidentified Richfield Oil Company tanker waits at Berth 57 to load a cargo of crude. By 1925, the company's shipments totaled more than 601,000 tons valued at more than $7.6 million, or more than 50 percent of both the tonnage and valuation of all commerce moving through the port. Founded in 1905, the Richfield Oil Company was one of the first oil enterprises to operate terminal facilities at the port and today is one of the port's oldest tenant partners. In the late 1950s, the company successfully drilled the first commercial oil well in Alaska. From that point, its shipping fleet was mainly engaged in carrying crude from Alaska to refineries at Long Beach and several other ports in California. The company merged with the Atlantic Refining Company in 1966 to form Atlantic Richfield, most commonly known as ARCO, and is now one of the largest oil companies in the world. (Courtesy of the Port of Long Beach Archive.)

Bulkhead Construction, 1929. Pilings frame the construction of the bulkhead at Berth 12 on Pier A. The wooden pilings would eventually be replaced with fireproof and rot-proof concrete substitutes in an ongoing effort to upgrade the port's docks and terminal facilities. (Courtesy of the Port of Long Beach Archive.)

More Rock, 1929. A Ford dump truck deposits a load of rock blasted from the Riverside quarry at one of the harbor's several ongoing development projects as one of the port's ubiquitous electric dredges works in the background. (Courtesy of the Port of Long Beach Archive.)

PIER 1, 1929. Construction began on Municipal Pier 1, which was built as part of an effort to centralize the port's cargo-handling activity away from Piers A and B and into the port's Inner Harbor. (Courtesy of the Port of Long Beach Archive.)

STEAM POWER, 1929. As the boss and foreman survey their work, a gang of laborers assists at one of the port's many construction sites. Here a high-voltage power line is laid under one of the harbor's several channels. (Courtesy of the Port of Long Beach Archive.)

Last Lady Afloat, 1930. The *Lumber Lady* was built during World War I and served as a lumber carrier along the Pacific Coast until the mid-1950s when she was sold for scrap. The ship made frequent calls at the Port of Long Beach and was the last steam schooner privately operated by a West Coast lumber company. (Courtesy of the author's collection.)

Pacific Coast Service, 1930. An unidentified Coastwise Line ship unloads her cargo. Coastwise ships called at Berth 7 on Pier A carrying a variety of intracoastal cargoes, from canned salmon to sewing machines, on the route linking Long Beach with San Francisco, Portland, Seattle, and Alaska. (Courtesy of the Port of Long Beach Archive.)

Rail Access, 1930. A track gang works on installing a switch on a rail line near one of the port's terminals. The upswing in cargo volume moving through the Port of Long Beach made improved rail access a critical tool in attracting industries and business. At the time, both the Union Pacific and the Pacific Electric served the port. (Courtesy of the Port of Long Beach Archive.)

San Pedro Bay, 1930. An interesting map of San Pedro Bay shows the adjacent ports of Long Beach and Los Angeles. By this time, both ports had become major challengers to the West Coast cargo supremacy of San Francisco Bay and Puget Sound. (Courtesy of the Port of Long Beach Archive.)

ECONOMIC ENGINE, 1930. The port handled 4.1 million tons of cargo in 1931, a surge of almost 40 percent over the 1.1 million tons that passed over the port's docks five years earlier. The port found itself fast becoming a critical component of Southern California's rapidly growing economy. (Courtesy of the Port of Long Beach Archive.)

PILINGS, 1930. Thousands of wooden pilings were needed to feed the continued construction and upgrading of the port's piers and docks. Most of the pilings were fabricated in the Pacific Northwest and then loaded aboard southbound coastal lumber steamers. (Courtesy of the Port of Long Beach Archive.)

PROCTOR AND GAMBLE, 1930. One of the largest industries to locate at the port was Proctor and Gamble, the Ohio-based manufacturer of household products such as soap, detergent, and other consumer goods. The company built a $5-million factory on 15 acres on Channel 2 at what is now the site of Pier C. (Courtesy of the author's collection.)

EARLY MULTIMODALISM, 1931. The Los Angeles–Long Beach Despatch Line offered door-to-door service moving cargo between the greater Los Angeles region and the San Francisco Bay Area using inland truck and rail connections to connect with a pair of coastal freighters. The Southern California hub for the operation was Berth 50 at the Port of Long Beach. (Courtesy of the Port of Long Beach Archive.)

PIER A CONSTRUCTION, 1931. A barge-mounted crane positions a boulder as part of the foundation of the extension of Pier A in the port's Middle Harbor. The same year, the Long Beach City Charter was amended to create a Harbor District, a Board of Harbor Commissioners, and a Harbor Department to control and manage operations at the port. (Courtesy of the Port of Long Beach Archive.)

LUMBER SCHOONERS, 1931. Lumber to fuel the explosive growth of Southern California remained a staple of the port's master cargo manifest in the decades preceding World War II. In 1926 alone, lumber accounted for one-quarter of the total value of cargo moving through the port. One of the tireless fleet of lumber schooners that called at the port is seen docked at Berth 50, Pier 1. (Courtesy of the Port of Long Beach Archive.)

Home Port, 1931. Several ships of the U.S. Pacific Fleet, including battleships, heavy cruisers, destroyers, tenders, and the aircraft carriers *Saratoga* and *Lexington*, ride at anchor outside the recently completed breakwater. Virtually all of the ships in this image saw active service in World War II with some, including the *Lexington*, lost in action. (Courtesy of the Port of Long Beach Archive.)

Muddy Work, 1931. Two mud-spattered port engineers prepare to survey a construction site at the port. The vagaries of nature and the demands of forecasted cargo growth gave the Port of Long Beach's understaffed port engineering department little time to focus on anything other than work. (Courtesy of the Port of Long Beach Archive.)

HEAVY CRUISER, 1932. A crowd waits as the crew of the heavy cruiser USS *Chicago* prepares to disembark at the port. This year, the Port of Long Beach became the home port for the *Chicago* and more than 50 capital and auxiliary ships of the U.S. Pacific Fleet, including the battleships *Arizona*, *Pennsylvania*, *Nevada*, and *Colorado*. (Courtesy of the Port of Long Beach Archive.)

CANNERIES, 1933. Before the construction of the U.S. Naval Shipyard on Terminal Island, commercial fishing operations, both large and small, used the island as their base of operations. Among the fish-canning companies with operations on the island at the time were the South Pacific Canning Company and the Long Beach Tuna Canning Company, which later changed its name to Chicken of the Sea. (Courtesy of the Port of Long Beach Archive.)

HARBOR STAFF, 1932. Port of Long Beach manager James Collins (back row, left) and Capt. C. E. Barry, traffic manager (back row, right), are joined by three port staff members on the front steps of the Long Beach Harbor Department administration building. (Courtesy of the Port of Long Beach Archive.)

FLEET ANCHORAGE, 1935. Eleven capital ships, including the battleships *Arizona*, *Pennsylvania*, and *California*, can be seen in this aerial image of the port. The world-famous Pike, a popular amusement spot for fleet sailors on liberty, can be seen on the shoreline at center left. (Courtesy of the Port of Long Beach Archive.)

STEVEDORES, 1935. Two Metropolitan Stevedore Company workers are seen here with a suction vacuum used to unload copra from ships' holds. The company was one of the first at the port to offer specialized cargo-handling capability and still conducts cargo-handling operations at several of the port's terminals. (Courtesy of the Port of Long Beach Archive.)

SOAP MANUFACTURING, 1935. Proctor and Gamble built a production facility on 15 acres sited along the 200-foot-wide Cerritos Channel. The plant employed 1,200 people during the tough Depression years and can be seen in the foreground with the port's Inner Harbor in the distance. (Courtesy of the Port of Long Beach Archive.)

A Dane Calls, 1936. The trade routes linking the Port of Long Beach and Europe grew in importance during the years leading up to World War II. Here the Danish-flag *Nordnap* is eased from her Pier 1 berth on the Cerritos Channel, outbound for the Panama Canal and home. (Courtesy of the Port of Long Beach Archive.)

Municipal Pier, 1937. This aerial image shows the development of Municipal Pier 1, the heart of the port's cargo-handling activity in the prewar years. Much of the 20 million tons of cargo handled at the port during the year moved across the wooden structure. (Courtesy of the Port of Long Beach Archive.)

Black Gold, 1938. Oil was discovered underneath port property in a major development that would have a long-term economic and infrastructural impact on the port for decades to come. The find dovetailed with the discovery, 17 years prior, of oil in the nearby community of Signal Hill. Over the years, oil has become a staple of the port's annual cargo volume. Much of the crude that passes through the port originates in the North Slope region of Alaska. Currently the port is the favored West Coast oil harbor because it is the only one that has the capability of handling the latest generation of supertankers. The ARCO terminal at the port sits on a 76-foot-deep channel from which a 30-inch pipeline carries the crude directly to the company's nearby refinery. Berth 121 and Berth 78 at the port are run by British Petroleum and are linked by pipeline to a refinery in nearby Carson, while the oil facility at Berth 86 is operated by Shell. (Courtesy of the Port of Long Beach Archive.)

American-Hawaiian Steamship Company, 1938. The freighter *Missourian* loads cargo at her berth on Pier A. Despite its name, the American-Hawaiian Steamship Company focused primarily on providing intercoastal service between ports on the U.S. Atlantic and Pacific Coasts, as well as regular sailings on several foreign trade routes. The company ceased operations in 1956. (Courtesy of the Port of Long Beach Archive.)

Transit Shed, 1938. Pyramids of imported bagged cargo dominate the interior of a transit shed at the port as they await inspection and clearance through U.S. Customs. Tea and spices from Ceylon, India, and Madagascar, as well as coffee from Central America and Brazil, were among the most common bagged imports moving through the port. (Courtesy of the Port of Long Beach Archive.)

DOCK WORK, 1938. The *Coast Beaver,* operated by the San Francisco–based Coastwise Line, rides high in the water while she awaits cargo for San Francisco and points north at Pier A on the Cerritos Channel. The port's water taxi landing can be seen in the foreground. (Courtesy of the Port of Long Beach Archive.)

WAREHOUSE CONSTRUCTION, 1938. Pier A's capacity to handle a wider variety of cargo was significantly enhanced with the construction of a new concrete and steel-framed warehouse, the first on the pier. The completely enclosed structure was completed the following year. (Courtesy of the Port of Long Beach Archive.)

KINGFISHER FLYOVER, 1939. Pictured here is a navy OS2U "Kingfisher" scouting aircraft on a training flight over the port. This aircraft, attached to the battleship USS *Pennsylvania*, normally operated as a catapult-launched floatplane, but has been refitted with landing gear to temporarily fly from Reeves Field Naval Air Station on Terminal Island while her mother ship undergoes minor repairs at the Long Beach Navy Yard. (Courtesy of the Port of Long Beach Archive.)

MOORE-MCCORMACK LINE, 1938. One of the leading U.S. flag carriers to South America and, from 1926 on, the leading U.S. flag carrier to Scandinavia and the Baltic, Moore-McCormack's parent company diversified over the years into other fields. Here the *Mormacstar* unloads bags of Brazilian coffee on Pier A. (Courtesy of the Port of Long Beach Archive.)

PORT STAFF, 1939. The end of the Depression was dimmed by the dark clouds of war as the decade of the 1930s came to a close. Under the leadership of newly appointed general manager Eloi J. Amar (front row, fifth from left), the people in this image laid the foundation for the development of the Port of Long Beach into a world-class harbor complex. Amar—nicknamed "Frenchy"—served as president of the Los Angeles Harbor Commission before he accepted the post of general manager of the Long Beach Harbor Department. The cigar-chomping Amar, a native of nearby San Pedro, served in the top post at the port for 19 years and led the port through some of its most challenging, and rewarding, times. He retired in 1958. (Courtesy of the Port of Long Beach Archive.)

Three

"AMERICA'S MOST MODERN PORT"

With the acquisition of 100 acres of land on the Long Beach side of Terminal Island in 1940, Congress approved Public Law 667, which authorized the U.S. Navy to begin construction of a naval dockyard at the Port of Long Beach. For the next four decades, the port became a major repair and logistics base for the U.S. Pacific Fleet.

Work on the San Pedro Bay breakwater was suspended due to World War II, with construction resuming in 1946 and completed three years later. In 1949, the port became the first in the Western Hemisphere to utilize a land-based radar system to guide ships in and out of the harbor.

Oil production surged at the port during the war, with 126 rigs pumping 17,000 barrels a day for $10 million in annual revenues.

But the blessing also turned out to be a major headache for the port. The oil drilling that had produced so much revenue also caused serious problems with subsidence, the sinking of large tracts of ground due to petroleum extraction. This situation called for the construction of dikes to control massive flooding of the port's Inner and Outer Harbor facilities at high tide.

The problem was so severe that *Time* magazine went so far as to call Long Beach "America's Sinking City," because of the dramatic lowering and sinking of the ground around the port.

The silver lining of the subsidence was that it had helped create a deepwater harbor ready to accommodate the newer, larger ships that were being put into service in the surging transpacific trades.

As a result, the expensive dredging need to deepen the channels at the rival Port of Los Angeles was not necessary at Long Beach. This permitted in the 1950s and early 1960s the earmarking of major investments in the new terminal facilities that would lay the foundation for the port becoming a major global player in the coming conversion of containerized cargo.

Trade with the Far East soared. Japan alone, for example, saw its export volume grow fivefold from $259 million in 1948 to more than $1.3 billion in 1953, with a significant amount of it moving through the Port of Long Beach.

Under the leadership of general managers Eloi Amar and Charles Vickers, "America's Sinking City" became "America's Most Modern Port," world class in its own right and no longer Los Angeles's neighboring little sister.

NAVAL SHIPYARD, 1940. The U.S. Navy acquired 119 acres of land on the Long Beach side of Terminal Island for $1. The site was developed into one of the largest naval support facilities and shipyards in the country and continued in operation until it was closed by the government in 1997. (Courtesy of the Port of Long Beach Archive.)

NEUTRAL COLORS, 1940. The freighter *Doña Nati* has large U.S. flags painted on her sides in an effort to broadcast her status as a ship sailing under the flag of a neutral nation during a time of war. The practice was common from 1939 to December 1941, when the United States entered World War II. (Courtesy of the Port of Long Beach Archive.)

SHIP PILOTS, 1940. Founded by Capt. Jacob Jacobsen, the Jacobsen Pilot Service has served at the Port of Long Beach since 1924. In 1949, the company made history when it became the first pilotage service in the world to operate a shore-based radar system to guide ships into and out of a deepwater port. (Courtesy of the Port of Long Beach Archive.)

ALWAYS MORE LUMBER, 1940. Several nondescript steamers unload their deck cargoes of milled Pacific Northwest and British Columbian lumber at the port's Municipal Dock. Much of the wood would be used in the construction of thousands of homes throughout Southern California. (Courtesy of the Port of Long Beach Archive.)

HEAVY LIFT CONSTRUCTION, 1940. Much of the heavy-duty work at the port was done by the Pacific Towboat and Salvage Company. At right, a heavy lift crane takes a brief break, while a smaller crane builds up a head of steam. (Courtesy of the Port of Long Beach Archive.)

PORT PILOT, 1940. Long Beach port pilot Thomas Thorley stands on the foredeck of the pilot boat *Polarus III* holding a portable radio-telephone, which gave him the capability of ship-to-shore communication. Thorley would later serve as general manager of the port from 1964 to 1977. (Courtesy of the Port of Long Beach Archive.)

LAST CALL, 1940. A sleek Italian-flag freighter makes her last call at the Port of Long Beach in late December. A little more than a year later, the United States would be at war with Italy and her allies, Germany and Japan. (Courtesy of the Port of Long Beach Archive.)

NEW LAUNCH, 1941. A few months before the Japanese attack on Pearl Harbor, the Consolidated Steel Corporation took over the operations of the Craig shipyard. The C-1–type freighter *Agwiprince* was one of the first ships launched under the yard's new management. The ship was built for the Atlantic, Gulf, and West Indies Steamship Company. (Courtesy of the Port of Long Beach Archive.)

AMERICA CALLS, 1941. A crowd gathers as the United States Lines's superliner *America* called at the Port of Long Beach. The ship, built a year earlier by the Newport News Shipbuilding and Drydock Company, sported prewar neutrality markings and was the largest merchant ship to visit the port up to that time. (Courtesy of the Port of Long Beach Archive.)

OIL WELLS, 1943. More than 125 wells on port property were drilling full-time for crude oil when this image was exposed. During the peak war years, the wells were pumping more than 17,000 barrels of oil daily, generating more than $10 million in revenues to fund port development projects. (Courtesy of the Port of Long Beach Archive.)

Key Logistics Hub, 1944. "Victory is dependent upon the solution of the logistics problem," wrote Gen. Douglas MacArthur in the summer of 1942. Part of that solution was provided by the Port of Long Beach, which played a key role as one of the nation's most important, and busiest, logistical bases. During the war years, every conceivable classification of cargo from food, clothing, tanks, ammunition, trucks, jeeps, crated aircraft, potable water, aviation gasoline, spare engine parts, and artillery pieces moved from factories and depots across the country to the port's docks to be loaded aboard thousands of ships and carried across the vast expanses of the Pacific theatre of operations. Haze gray–painted cargo ships, ready to sail under sealed orders for undisclosed destinations, wait for longshoremen to load their outbound cargo from Southern Pacific boxcars spotted on dockside tracks. (Courtesy of the Port of Long Beach Archive.)

Liberty Ship, 1944. With her name board covered over for security purposes, a Liberty-type freighter with a deck load of PT boats and outsize crates destined for the South Pacific called at the port for minor repairs. Many of the Liberty- and Victory-type freighters that visited Long Beach were built at nearby shipyards in San Pedro and Wilmington. (Courtesy of the Port of Long Beach Archive.)

Pier Fire, 1945. Wreathed in acrid smoke, the City of Long Beach fireboat *Petrel*, the U.S. Navy yard tug YTB 511, the Long Beach Harbor Department Harbor Taxi 11, and several other craft direct their water monitors on a blaze that broke out near several tankers and other ships berthed at the Long Beach Naval Shipyard. (Courtesy of the Port of Long Beach Archive.)

War-Weary Flattop, 1945. A few weeks after the end of the war, an unidentified 27,000-ton Essex-class aircraft carrier can be seen tied up at the Long Beach Naval Shipyard as a line of buses in the foreground wait to carry her eager crew to a processing center for discharge and a return to civilian life. Her flight deck bare of aircraft, the ship is finally at ease after months of combat in the Pacific. (Courtesy of the Port of Long Beach Archive.)

A Forest of Derricks, 1946. Almost nonstop oil drilling over a period of many years on port property was the primary cause of major shifts in the makeup of the land under the port. Major flooding and land displacement were the main results of a condition that would plague the port into the 1960s. (Courtesy of the Port of Long Beach Archive.)

NAVY YARD, 1946. Two years after the end of the war, dozens of U.S. Navy ships are gathered at the Long Beach Naval Shipyard and at anchor in the port's Middle Harbor awaiting final disposition. The ships will be reconditioned for active duty, placed in reserve, sold for civilian use, or scrapped. (Courtesy of the Port of Long Beach Archive.)

EAST ASIATIC COMPANY, 1946. By the end of the year, the port had completed the construction of nine clear-span transit sheds on Pier F. At her berth at the pier, the 9,900-ton, Danish-flag motor ship *Korea* loads steel sheets for export. The ship sailed under the house flag of the East Asiatic Company and was eventually scrapped in Hong Kong in 1967. (Courtesy of the Port of Long Beach Archive.)

PIGGYBACK CARGO, 1946. A barge-mounted heavy lift crane muscles an 82-foot U.S. Coast Guard cutter onto the foredeck of the Liberty-type freighter *Governor Dixon* for shipment through the Panama Canal to New Orleans. Bearing a U.S. flag, the cargo ship was operated by the Waterman Steamship Company. (Courtesy of the Port of Long Beach Archive.)

MOVING THE "GOOSE," 1946. Components of Howard Hughes's massive H-4 "Hercules" flying boat slowly inch toward Pier E, where they will be assembled into the largest aircraft ever built to date. The all-wood aircraft is still known as the "Spruce Goose" despite the fact that it does not have a single piece of spruce in its entire structure. (Courtesy of the Port of Long Beach Archive.)

The "Goose" Takes Wing, 1947. Howard Hughes silenced his detractors when he taxied the massive, eight-engine H-4 flying boat from its hangar on Pier E into the port's Outer Harbor for its one—and only—flight. A navy helicopter and a heavy cruiser provide a background to the historic event. (Courtesy of the Port of Long Beach Archive.)

Wave Action, 1947. Subsidence caused by oil drilling was not the only natural force faced by the port. A crane repositions rock on a jetty to counter the force of ocean waves that perennially crash into the port's exposed position on San Pedro Bay. (Courtesy of the Port of Long Beach Archive.)

"HERMAN THE GERMAN," 1948. In 1941, the Germans built three giant cranes to lift, repair, and overhaul U-boats. All three survived the war with England, Russia, and the United States, each claiming one as war reparations. The Russians took theirs apart, but were unable to reassemble it, while the crane claimed by the British capsized and sank in the English Channel. The 385-ton, self-propelled crane claimed by the United States was towed from Bremerhaven, through the Panama Canal to Long Beach, where it was put in service carrying out a multitude of heavy-lift duties at the Long Beach Naval Shipyard.

Christened "Herman the German," the crane carried out a variety of heavy-lift jobs at the shipyard, from replacing the 16-inch rifles on the battleship *New Jersey* to manhandling the "Spruce Goose" in October 1980 onto a waiting barge for a move to its new home adjacent to the *Queen Mary* on Pier J. The crane, officially known as YD-171, was, at the time, the largest floating crane in the world. (Courtesy of the author's collection.)

NEW FACILITIES, 1948. A tug assists an unidentified, Liberty-type U.S. Navy transport as she maneuvers in the port's Turning Basin. Workers in the foreground direct a tractor-mounted construction crane involved in one of the many projects underway at the port in the years following the end of the war. (Courtesy of the Port of Long Beach Archive.)

BULK LOADER, 1948. Construction was completed on the modern terminal on Pier D to handle shipments of a variety of bulk commodities, from grain and nitrates to copra and salt. Today Metropolitan Stevedore is the leading bulk-terminal operator at the port. (Courtesy of the Port of Long Beach Archive.)

PACIFIC QUEEN, 1948. The three-masted ship was towed to the port to serve as a museum in a plan that never materialized. Built as the *Balclutha* in Scotland in 1886, the ship returned to the Bay Area in 1954, where she was restored to her former name and glory and given a permanent berth at the National Maritime Museum in San Francisco. (Courtesy of the Port of Long Beach Archive.)

PIER A, 1948. Like a forest in the distance, seemingly countless oil wells provide a backdrop to a variety of export cargo on Pier A sorted and waiting to be loaded onto outbound freighters. (Courtesy of the Port of Long Beach Archive.)

POSTWAR AID, 1949. The European Recovery Program, known famously as the Marshall Plan, was crafted to restore the economy of war-ravaged Europe. From 1949 to 1951, more than $13 billion in aid, from agricultural equipment and raw materials to fertilizer and animal feed, was shipped from the United States to Germany, France, Austria, Belgium, Italy, England, the Netherlands, Greece, and 10 other countries in Western Europe. Of all the monies allotted, by mid-1951, $3.4 billion had been spent on U.S. exports of raw materials and semi-manufactured products; $3.2 billion on food, feed, and fertilizer; $1.9 billion on machines, vehicles, and equipment; and $1.6 billion on fuel such as coal, diesel fuel, heating oil, and gasoline. The plan proved to be a boon to U.S. ports and Long Beach was no exception. Here the Liberty-type freighter *Wallace R. Farrington* lists to starboard as she loads a relief cargo of coal for delivery to the Port of Rotterdam. (Courtesy of the Port of Long Beach Archive.)

Dock Development, 1948. Work continues on the construction of Pier E, which adds an additional 36 acres of cargo-handling space to the port's Outer Harbor. At the same time, Pier B in the port's Inner Harbor is doubled in size. (Courtesy of the Port of Long Beach Archive.)

Steel Exports, 1949. An unidentified Luckenbach Steamship Company freighter berthed at Pier D loads an intercoastal bulk cargo, while a steel shipment in the foreground is marked for loading aboard the Isbrandtsen Steamship Company's cargo ship, *Flying Dragon*. (Courtesy of the Port of Long Beach Archive.)

OIL PIPELINE, 1949. Sections of steel pipe are loaded aboard the Pacific Far East Line freighter *F. J. Luckenbach* for shipment to Saudi Arabia. The pipe was slated for use in the construction of an oil refinery being built by ARAMCO. (Courtesy of the Port of Long Beach Archive.)

SUBSIDENCE DAMAGE, 1949. Hundreds of acres of port property were flooded when subsidence caused large portions of land to drop about six feet. Tidal action, pumping and improving the effectiveness of the port's system of bulkheads, provided what would be only temporary relief from the chronic problem. (Courtesy of the Port of Long Beach Archive.)

Soap for Export, 1949. Protected from the elements, palletized boxes of Ivory and Camay hand soap and Duz laundry detergent await shipment in a Pier F transit shed. The soap was manufactured at the Proctor and Gamble plant, located on Pier C on the Cerritos Channel. (Courtesy of the Port of Long Beach Archive.)

Cement Exports, 1950. Work began in the spring on a new terminal equipped with a bulk loader for outbound shipments of cement. The new facility was located at Berth 208 on Pier F. California has led the nation in the production of cement since the 1950s, with a large percentage of the cement bound for overseas markets moving through the Port of Long Beach. (Courtesy of the Port of Long Beach Archive.)

CALIFORNIA COTTON, 1950. Cotton was, and continues to be, an important export commodity at the Port of Long Beach. In the postwar years, California-grown cotton was a major U.S. export to Japan, which, at the time, transformed a majority of it into the textiles that made up one-half of that country's total exports. (Courtesy of the Port of Long Beach Archive.)

DOCK DAMAGE, 1950. Subsidence continued to plague the port through the 1950s. Here the tug *Resolute* ties up at one of the port's piers, which has its apron bowed by the erosion caused by nonstop oil drilling eating away at the foundation underneath its support pilings. (Courtesy of the Port of Long Beach Archive.)

OUTBOUND ORANGES, 1950. A load of Sunkist oranges is prepared for loading aboard an unidentified freighter for shipment to the Far East. More than 100 years old, the Southern California–based agricultural co-op has traditionally exported between 25 and 30 percent of its citrus products every year, much of it through the port. (Courtesy of the Port of Long Beach Archive.)

NATURE'S WORK, 1950. While the breakwater protects the port from storm damage, over the years, heavy waves created by the many frequent storms that have lashed San Pedro Bay have destroyed many seaside cottages and businesses adjacent to the port. The fall storm that caused this damage reportedly lasted three days. (Courtesy of the Port of Long Beach Archive.)

DREDGING, 1951. The Puget Sound Bridge and Dredging Company carried out some of the most difficult dredging projects at the port in the postwar years. The dredge *H. W. McCurdy*, one of the company's largest high-powered suction dredges, can be seen tied up to the dock in the port's Inner Harbor. (Courtesy of the Port of Long Beach Archive.)

PILE DRIVING, 1951. A new pile is driven to strengthen the foundation of a new transit shed at the port. The remedial work was done to correct the severe damage to the port's docks and piers caused by subsidence. (Courtesy of the Port of Long Beach Archive.)

Bulk Loading, 1952. The *Azumasan Maru* waits at Pier D to load a bulk shipment of fertilizer pellets for shipment to Japan. The Mitsui Line freighter served in the transpacific trades and was a frequent visitor to the port. (Courtesy of the Port of Long Beach Archive.)

Official Visit, 1952. California governor Goodwin Knight (right) visited the port in recognition of its increasingly important role as a driver of the state's increasingly international economy. As a young man, Knight combined stints as a newspaper reporter, grocery clerk, and hard-rock miner with service in the navy and studies at Stanford and Cornell Universities prior to entering his chosen field of law. (Courtesy of the Port of Long Beach Archive.)

Lumber Imports, 1952. Southern California's booming housing market made lumber a prime commodity at the Port of Long Beach in the postwar years. Much of the cut lumber moving through the port was handled on Pier A and was shipped in from the U.S. Pacific Northwest and Canada. (Courtesy of the Port of Long Beach Archive.)

Inner Harbor, 1953. Five freighters work at Berths 5–10 on Pier A. States Marine Lines, which offered regular service between the U.S. West Coast and the Far East, based its operations at the port at the huge transit shed in the foreground. (Courtesy of the Port of Long Beach Archive.)

TRUCK CARGO, 1953. A truck is loaded at the transit shed on Pier A. Import cargo for consignees in Southern California moved by truck, while the three railroads that served the port moved goods and commodities to points throughout the United States. (Courtesy of the Port of Long Beach Archive.)

***PASADENA* IN LONG BEACH, 1953.** The East Asiatic Company cargo ship *Pasadena* tied up at Berth 3 on Pier A. The Danish-flagship sailed on the company's route linking the West Coast of North America with ports in Northern Europe. (Courtesy of the Port Of Long Beach Archive.)

POSTWAR LIBERTIES, 1954. The end of World War II found the United States operating the largest merchant fleet in the world. Thousands of cargo ships were built that survived for many years after the end of hostilities, including hundreds of Liberty-type freighters built at shipyards around the country. Many of the Liberties were "sold foreign" and operated under the flags of a number of countries including France, Italy, Norway, and Greece. The tramp freighter *Pacificus* (seen above) sailed under the Greek flag and called at the Port of Long Beach several times during the 1950s. Built as the *Lucien Labaudt* at the Permanente Metals Corporation shipyard in Richmond, California, in late 1944, the ship sailed under a total of four other names during her career before she was scrapped in Kaohsiung, Taiwan, in 1969 after 25 hard years at sea. (Courtesy of the Port of Long Beach Archive.)

NEWSPRINT, 1953. Virtually all of the newsprint used by newspapers throughout Southern California and elsewhere is imported from Canada, with some coming from as far away as Finland and the Baltic. Rolled newsprint is seen here ready for shipment by truck and rail to waiting printing presses. (Courtesy of the Port of Long Beach Archive.)

MORE OUTBOUND COTTON, 1954. Over the years, a significant amount of the cotton grown in California's fertile Central Valley has moved by rail or truck to the San Pedro Bay ports of Long Beach and Los Angeles for export to apparel mills in the Far East. Here two freighters use their shipboard booms to load baled and fumigated cotton into their holds. (Courtesy of the Port of Long Beach Archive.)

FIREBOAT CHRISTENING, 1954. The Long Beach City Fire Department has had the primary responsibility for fire safety at the port since its inception. This image shows LBFD and Long Beach harbor officials at the christening of the new Long Beach Fireboat No. 2. (Courtesy of the Port of Long Beach Archive.)

AUTO EXPORTS, 1954. In the years before international joint ventures and outsourcing, automobiles made in the United States were exported all over the world. In this image, a fleet of now-iconic Nash Metropolitans awaits loading onto a freighter for shipment overseas. (Courtesy of the Port of Long Beach Archive.)

PACIFIC CRUISING , 1954. On a hazy January morning, the Cunard Line passenger liner *Caronia*, assisted by a trio of Red Stack tugboats, glides into the port on the way to her berth. The ship was built in 1949 and was, at the time, the largest single-funneled ocean liner in the world. (Courtesy of the Port of Long Beach Archive.)

WHARF CONSTRUCTION, 1954. By the mid-1950s, workers had begun to replace most of the old wooden pilings supporting the port's wharves with new concrete structures. Here workmen put the finishing touches on the new pilings before the dock floor is laid. (Courtesy of the Port of Long Beach Archive.)

PACIFIC FAR EAST LINE, 1954. The Mariner-type freighter *Golden Bear* celebrates her maiden arrival at the Pacific Far East Line terminal on Pier A. The line operated on a route linking Southern California with Manila, San Fernando, Cebu, Iloilo, Hong Kong, Kobe, Nagoya, and Yokohama via San Francisco until it went out of business in 1979. (Courtesy of the Port of Long Beach Archive.)

RECORD CAR SHIPMENT, 1955. Like a tired, old dog lying next to her new litter of puppies, a Hansa Line freighter sits at her berth near the load of Volkswagens recently unloaded from her holds. The shipment was one of the first to bring the new VW from Germany to eager Southern California drivers. (Courtesy of the author's collection.)

CARGO UNDER CANVAS, 1955. A brief truck strike stranded tons of cargo on the port's docks, and the only remedy at the time was to store the freight under rented circus tents until the strike was settled. The cargo piles up as a harried cargo superintendent checks his manifest. (Courtesy of the Port of Long Beach Archive.)

DOCK ACTIVITY, 1955. While crated cargo is hoisted aboard the unidentified Victory-type freighter in the foreground, the Liberty-type cargo ship *Joel Chandler Harris* (center) and several other ships with their booms swung dockside are worked by gangs of longshoremen. (Courtesy of the Port of Long Beach Archive.)

STEEL SCRAP FOR EXPORT, 1955. The National Metal and Steel Corporation on Terminal Island processed countless tons of scrap metal during its 40 years of operation. Here a magnet loader is used to move a load of scrap metal from dockside gondola cars into the holds of the Greek-flag, Liberty-type freighter *Triton*. (Courtesy of the Port of Long Beach Archive.)

SUBSIDENCE, 1955. Worsening subsidence caused the ground to drop between 2 and 24 feet in an area covering more than 15 miles of port property. Despite the ongoing problem, a final solution to the subsidence issue would not be found for another 10 years. (Courtesy of the Port of Long Beach Archive.)

A Swedish Visitor, 1955. Bedecked with signal flags, the white-hulled passenger liner *Kungsholm* makes her first visit to the Port of Long Beach as a Red Stack tugboat eases the gleaming liner into her berth. The ship sailed under the Swedish-America Line house flag. (Courtesy of the Port of Long Beach Archive.)

World Trade Week, 1955. The port has observed World Trade Week every May since it became a national event in 1936. A 15-foot model of a modern cargo ship served as the centerpiece of the luncheon held at the port to celebrate the event. (Courtesy of the Port of Long Beach Archive.)

TRANSIT SHED CONSTRUCTION, 1956. The Liberty-type cargo ship *Transwestern* awaits her cargo and backdrops construction of one of the port's new steel-framed transit sheds. The sheds would continue to prove their value despite the introduction of containerization within a few years. (Courtesy of the Port of Long Beach Archive.)

CITRUS EXPORTS, 1956. Longshoremen at Berth 34 on Pier D prepare to load a shipment of California-grown oranges aboard an unidentified Norwegian-flag Westfal-Larsen Line freighter. The oranges were grown and processed by Sunkist and slated for shipment to ports in Northern Europe. (Courtesy of the Port of Long Beach Archive.)

Original Administration Building, 1956. The effects of subsidence can be dramatically seen in this image of the Long Beach Harbor Department headquarters. In four years, the port administrative staff would relocate to a new building on Harbor Plaza Drive. (Courtesy of the Port of Long Beach Archive.)

Orient Line, 1956. One of the world's most beautiful passenger liners, the buff-funneled *Orsova* was met by a huge crowd of spectators when she arrived on her maiden arrival at the port. The British-manned ship flew the house flag of the Orient Line. (Courtesy of the Port of Long Beach Archive.)

MORE SCRAP, 1956. Scrap metal continued to be a major export commodity moving through the port. Gondola cars filled with scrap bound for a steel mill in Japan line up dockside for unloading by a magnet crane into the hold of an American President Lines freighter. Much of the scrap exported from the port came from the ship-breaking activities at the nearby National Metal and Steel Corporation facility. (Courtesy of the Port of Long Beach Archive.)

FORD PLANT FIRE, 1956. Spectators on a highway overpass watch as a flotilla of Long Beach Fire Department, U.S. Navy, U.S. Coast Guard, and private-company tugs fight a fire that broke out in the paint shed of the Ford Motor Company factory at the port. The fire was kept from damaging the rest of the plant, which continued in operation until 1959. (Courtesy of the Port of Long Beach Archive.)

BALED COTTON, 1957. Baled cotton—fumigated and ready for shipment overseas—awaits loading into the holds of a waiting States Marine Lines cargo ship. An estimated 750,000 bales of cotton were exported from the Port of Long Beach during the year. The cotton was grown in California's fertile Central Valley and trucked to the port for processing and export. (Courtesy of the author's collection.)

JAPAN TRANSPORT, 1957. The white-hulled, C-3–type freighter *Japan Transport* sailed for the U.S.-flag Pacific Transport Lines on the route linking California with ports throughout the Far East. The line operated in conjunction with State Line and called at Berth 21 on Pier C. (Courtesy of the author's collection.)

DOCKSIDE LOADER, 1957. Ships calling at the port to load bulk cargoes such as fertilizer, borax, grain, or other commodities could be served by a rotary loader that emptied rail-hopper cars by turning them upside down so their contents were deposited onto a conveyor system that would carry the product into the ships' hold. (Courtesy of the Port of Long Beach Archive.)

BUNKERS, 1958. An unidentified freighter, its booms swung out to handle cargo, takes on bunker oil from a rail tank car dockside. The abundance of petroleum products made the harbor a popular port of call for ships needing to top off their fuel tanks. (Courtesy of the Port of Long Beach Archive.)

ISLAND COMPETITION, 1958. The Hawaiian Steamship Company was formed to compete with the well-established Matson Navigation Company on the lucrative route between California and Hawaii. The line operated three ships—the 12-passenger freighters *Kaimana* and *Lanikai* (above) and the 650-passenger liner *Leilani* (below), the former transatlantic liner *LaGuardia*. The new service was inaugurated in 1954 and failed four years later, with all three ships acquired by San Francisco–based American President Lines. The *Leilani*, built as a troopship in 1944, sailed for APL in the Pacific as the *President Roosevelt* and later served under several other names before going to the breakers yard in 2004. (Both, courtesy of the author's collection.)

FAREWELL "FRENCHY," 1958. City and port officials join to bid farewell to Aloi "Frenchy" Amar, who retired from his post as general manager after 19 years of service. Rarely seen without his trademark cigar, Amar (third from left) oversaw the operations of the port through the challenges of World War II, as well as its spectacular growth in the years immediately following the war. (Courtesy of the Port of Long Beach Archive.)

PIER E, 1959. A U.S. Navy tanker berthed in the foreground and the city of Long Beach in the background frame the port's Pier E complex on an exceptionally clear day. Pier E now serves as home to California United Terminals, which operates a 95-acre facility with five container cranes and 2,100 feet of berth space. (Courtesy of the Port of Long Beach Archive.)

CALMAR LINE, 1960. The *Seamar* works her cargo at Berths 24–25 on Pier E. The ship was equipped with its own onboard cranes and was one of six ships operated by the Calmar Lines on its intercoastal service carrying break-bulk and heavy-lift cargoes between California and ports on the U.S. East Coast via the Panama Canal. (Courtesy of the author's collection.)

OVERHEAD LIFT, 1960. A pair of dockside, whirly cranes works an unidentified break-bulk freighter at the port. Each as tall as a 10-story building with a capacity of 166,000 pounds, the 200-ton cranes moved on railroad tracks and could revolve 360 degrees. The cranes were used whenever a ship's onboard booms lacked the capacity to move heavy cargo into or out of its holds. (Courtesy of the Port of Long Beach Archive.)

NEW ADMINISTRATION BUILDING, 1960. The new seven-story building was constructed on Harbor Plaza Drive and officially dedicated on March 30. A large fresco that depicts the history of San Pedro Bay adorns the front of the building, which has, for more than four decades, centralized all of the port's administrative, management, and engineering operations. It is due for replacement by a larger, more environmentally friendly, structure on a 17-acre site just east of the present building by 2012. The plans for the new administration building maximize the use of natural light and provide amenities for the community such as public meeting rooms, a public cafeteria with outdoor access, an outdoor amphitheater, gardens for special functions, and a mile-long walking trail. The estimated cost of the new nine-story building and an adjacent parking structure will be $218 million. (Courtesy of the Port of Long Beach Archive.)

Four

A Global Port is Born

It was September 1962 when the containership *Elizabethport*, the largest cargo ship in the world at the time and the first containership to transit the Panama Canal, was gently eased into her berth at the new Sea-Land terminal on Pier G.

The Port of Long Beach would never be the same. Container cargo thereafter dominated the port's activities as the needs of shippers and the evolutionary development of more efficient logistics would combine to forge the port into a critical link in the global supply chain.

The expansion of both Pier J and Pier F, for example, was driven in large part by the increased volume of containers moving through the port. The project, begun in 1965 and completed six years later, required 3.4 million tons of rock and 30 million cubic yards of hydraulic fill to add 310 acres of terminal space to both piers. The pier expansion project was the largest of its kind in the world at the time.

In 1960, the Port of Long Beach initiated a major campaign—a $30-million water injection program dubbed Operation "Big Squirt"—to remediate the chronic problem of subsidence that had plagued the port for almost 30 years.

During the 1960s, the port also markedly improved its ability to handle the variety of other cargoes, from steel to coal, moving to and from markets all over the world. The Koppel Bulk Terminal on Pier A was the largest grain-loading facility on the U.S. West Coast when it was built in March 1962. The same year, the newly completed 23-acre auto facility on Pier E handled a record shipment of 1,152 Volkswagens from Germany.

It was during this period that the Port of Long Beach became a major player in the development of the "landbridge" method of moving container cargo—simply, the utilization of railcars to move containers to points across the country rather than relying on the traditional method of having ships transit the Panama Canal for direct calls at U.S. Gulf and East Coast ports.

Efforts to attract new business show fruition by 1971 as the port had almost achieved parity in cargo tonnage volume with the neighboring Port of Los Angeles. That year the Port of Long Beach handled 26.1 million tons of cargo, compared with 27 million handled by its San Pedro Bay neighbor.

CANBERRA, 1961. The twin-screw passenger liner *Canberra* was the largest British-flag passenger ship to be launched since the *Queen Elizabeth* was built in 1940. Homeported in Southhampton, England, the ship visited the port's Pier C terminal before departing for Australia on the next leg of her first round-the-world cruise. (Courtesy of the author's collection.)

LOADING BAGGAGE, 1961. Onboard overhead lifts are used to load baggage and supplies are loaded aboard the *Canberra* before she sails on her next transpacific voyage. The ship sailed for the fabled Peninsula and Orient Line (P&O) until 1997 when she was sold for $5 million and sent to a breakers yard in Pakistan. (Courtesy of the Port of Long Beach Archive.)

MANHATTAN ARRIVAL, 1961. The 951-foot tanker *Manhattan* was the largest tanker sailing under the U.S. flag. She was later fitted with an icebreaker bow, lengthened to over 1,000 feet, and had her deadweight increased by 9,000 tons to 151,500 tons before she made history in September 1969 by becoming the first merchant ship ever to traverse the ice-bound Northwest Passage. (Courtesy of the author's collection.)

***PRINCESS SOPHIE*, 1961.** Named for Princess Sophie of Greece, this 859-foot tanker was built by Bethlehem Steel's shipyard in Quincy, Massachusetts. The ship was chartered by the Atlantic Richfield Oil Company and was a regular visitor at the Port of Long Beach's oil terminal on the channel linking the Inner Harbor and Middle Harbor. (Courtesy of the author's collection.)

A New Age Dawns, 1962. Port general manager Charles Vickers addresses the crowd on hand to celebrate the arrival of the Sea-Land Service containership *Elizabethport*, the first ship of its kind to visit the Port of Long Beach. Over the following decades, container shipping eventually supplanted the more traditional, labor-intensive method of handling cargo, namely using shipboard equipment to load boxed, bagged, and barreled cargoes and stowing them loose in a ship's hold. Pioneered by Sea-Land Service, the Matson Navigation Company, and others, the development of containerization has dramatically reduced transportation costs, spurred the design of more efficient ships, ratchetted international trade to a level never seen before, and revolutionized the global economy. The historic event set the stage for the Port of Long Beach's development into one of the busiest container ports in the world. (Courtesy of the Port of Long Beach Archive.)

A Nuclear Visitor, 1962. The yacht-like NS *Savannah*, the only nuclear-powered merchant ship to ever fly the U.S. flag, visited the port on a goodwill tour to tout the use of atomic power for peaceful purposes. The cargo-passenger ship was managed by States Marine Lines and was only marginally successful as a commercial carrier before eventually being laid up in Norfolk, Virginia. (Courtesy of the author's collection.)

Container Pioneer, 1963. The only two container cranes at the port tower over the containership *Elizabethport*. With a capacity of 476 thirty-five-foot containers, the ship was one of four ships originally built as oil tankers during World War II, which Sea-Land Service converted into container carriers in the early 1960s. (Courtesy of the author's collection.)

AZALEA CITY, 1964. A converted C-2–type freighter, the *Azalea City* was one of a six-ship class of containerships initially operated by Sea-Land Service on a route linking the U.S. East and West Coasts. In 1999, Sea-Land Service was absorbed by Denmark's Maersk Line, which continues to call at its own 107-acre terminal on Pier J at the Port of Long Beach. (Courtesy of the author's collection.)

PIER J, 1965. Known as the "crab claw" for obvious reasons, Pier J was built on 310 acres of landfill to accommodate the larger containerships calling at the port. The job to build Pier J and Pier F required 3.4 million tons of rock and 30 million cubic yards of fill. At the time it was the world's largest port expansion project. (Courtesy of the Port of Long Beach Archive.)

STATES LINE, 1965. Sporting the States Line "sea horse" logo on her funnel, the freighter *Colorado* is seen outbound from the Port of Long Beach for San Francisco. The ship was one of four conventional cargo liners that the company sailed on the route linking California with Japan, Korea, and Taiwan, until it ceased operations in 1979. (Courtesy of the author's collection.)

GERMAN TO GERMAN, 1965. Long Beach–based YD-171, the giant "Herman the German," lifts a luxury yacht aboard the cargo liner *Riederstein* for shipment to Denmark. The cargo liner sailed under the colors of North German Lloyd and was sold to the competing Hapag-Lloyd shipping line in 1970. (Courtesy of the Port of Long Beach Archive.)

KEYSTONE STATE, 1965. States Marine Lines (not to be confused with its competitor, States Line) offered service connecting the port with the Far East. The C-4–type freighter *Keystone State* is seen tied up awaiting a cargo at Berth 10 on Pier A. (Courtesy of the Port of Long Beach Archive.)

STANDARD FRUIT, 1966. The Vaccaro Brothers refrigerated fruit carrier in the foreground unloads bananas at the port. The company had operated as the Standard Fruit and Steamship Company since 1924 and was eventually acquired by the Castle and Cooke Corporation, which became the Dole Food Company in 1991. (Courtesy if the Port of Long Beach Archive.)

TUG LIFT, 1967. The U.S. Coast Guard yard tug *Bollard* is lifted aboard the heavy-lift ship *Transcolumbia* for shipment to her new homeport of New London, Connecticut. Two barges have already been loaded onto the foredeck of the specially equipped ship, which was operated by Hudson Waterways. (Courtesy of the author's collection.)

TERMINAL ISLAND LINK, 1967. The unfinished Gerald Desmond Bridge looms over the U.S. Navy tanker *Mispillion* (AO-105). The four-lane arch bridge gives a 155-foot clearance over the Cerritos Channel and links Long Beach with Terminal Island. The span was named after a former City of Long Beach district attorney. (Courtesy of the author's collection.)

THE QUEEN ARRIVES, 1967. Escorted by four U.S. Navy minesweepers and gaggle of small craft, the RMS *Queen Mary* arrives at the port for eventual conversion into a hotel and museum. The classic liner, launched in 1936, is considered by many to be one of the most beautiful ships ever built. (Courtesy of the author's collection.)

THUMS ISLAND, 1967. Three soundproof, pastel-color oil rigs sprout on Thum's Island, a man-made oil facility adjacent to the port's Pier J. The name of the island is an acronym for the consortium of oil companies that were contracted to operate the wells—Texaco, Humble (now Exxon), Union, Mobil, and Shell. (Courtesy of the Port of Long Beach Archive.)

UNITED STATES LINES, 1967. An unidentified United States Lines containership loads 40-foot containers, or "cans" as they were known, at the carrier's terminal at Berth 230 on Pier G. At left center, the new port administration building, literally, oversees several new terminal and transshipment facility projects. (Courtesy of the Port of Long Beach Archive.)

BULK TERMINAL, 1968. The bulk carrier *Conqueror Bulker* waits to load a grain cargo at the Koppel Bulk Terminal on Pier F. When originally built, the $2.8-million facility was the largest grain-loading terminal on the Pacific Coast. The facility changed hands when Koppel was acquired in 1979 by Agrex Inc., a subsidiary of Japan's Mitsubishi Corporation. (Courtesy of the author's collection.)

The Queen Converted, 1968. Prior to her being permanently berthed as a museum ship on Pier J, the liner *Queen Mary* underwent an extensive overhaul at the Long Beach Naval Shipyard. Work included removal of all the ship's boiler rooms, the forward engine room, both turbo-generator rooms, and the freeing of internal spaces for restaurants, retail businesses, and historic exhibits. (Courtesy of the Port of Long Beach Archive.)

The Queen at Rest, 1969. The *Queen Mary* at her permanent berth on Pier J is pictured here. This image shows the ship before the geodesic dome was built near her stern to house a museum and exhibit the gigantic HK-1 "Spruce Goose" flying boat. (Courtesy of the Port of Long Beach Archive.)

Copra Cargo, 1969. Copra is the dried meat of coconuts and is produced in Asia and the South Pacific. Shipped in bulk, the commodity is used in a variety of products from cosmetics to cattle feed. Here a small tractor is used to position a load of copra for off-loading from the hold of a freighter docked at the port. (Courtesy of the Port of Long Beach Archive.)

American Astronaut, 1970. One of the first containerships built for United States Lines, the *American Astronaut* sailed on the lines' transpacific route between the U.S. West Coast and the Far East. The most recognized U.S.-flag steamship company for decades, the company, sadly, was formally liquidated in 1992 after 71 years of service. (Courtesy of the author's collection.)

MAIDEN ARRIVAL, 1971. Decked out with her entire inventory of signal flags, the tanker *ARCO Prudhoe Bay* made her first visit to the port. The 70,378-deadweight-ton ship has a capacity of 478,000 barrels of petroleum products and made the visit shortly after she went into service for Long Beach–headquartered ARCO Marine. (Courtesy of the author's collection.)

KOREA SHIPPING CORPORATION, 1971. The standard cargo freighter *Korean Frontier* is nudged into her berth by a Red Stack tugboat. Korea Shipping was one of the first Korean shipping firms to achieve prominence in the postwar years, but the company was slow to adapt to container technology and was eventually absorbed by the giant Hanjin Shipping Company in 1988. (Courtesy of the Port of Long Beach Archive.)

LOADING CARS, 1972. Roll-on/roll-off ship technology was just taking hold when this image was taken of a pair of Chevrolet pickup trucks being loaded in the traditional manner into the cargo spaces of an unidentified break-bulk ship for shipment overseas. Because of the new technology, within a few years the port would become one of the country's busiest auto ports. (Courtesy of the author's collection.)

A GIANT ARRIVES, 1973. A gantry crane awaits the docking of the Sea-Land Service containership *Sea-Land McLean* at her berth on Pier G. The giant, European-built, diesel-powered SL-7-class ship and her seven sisters could maintain 33 knots, 10–15 knots faster than any other cargo ship then sailing on the world's trade routes.

MYSTERY SHIP, 1974. The deep-sea exploration ship *Hughes Glomar Explorer* was built by the reclusive Howard Hughes to search for deep-sea oil deposits. In reality, the ship, based in Long Beach, was used to carry out several classified operations for the U.S. intelligence community, including the recovery of the fore section of a Russian nuclear submarine, which accidentally sank off the Hawaiian Islands. (Courtesy of the Port of Long Beach Archive.)

RED STAR ARRIVAL, 1974. Under the watchful eye of the Coast Guard, the Soviet technical research ship *Rainbow* called at the port on a goodwill visit. The visit took place at the height of the Cold War, when the terms "technical research" and "goodwill visit" could have a variety of potentially sinister definitions. (Courtesy of the Port of Long Beach Archive.)

Five

The Port Grows and "Greens"

The 1970s and 1980s firmly planted the Port of Long Beach's claim to being one of the most modern ports in the world.

As early as 1973, the port was recognized for its efforts to improve and protect its environment. That year, the American Association of Port Authorities awarded the port its Environmental "E" Award in recognition of its advances in oil spill prevention and control, vessel traffic control, and mitigating air pollution.

Long Beach was also the first port in the Western Hemisphere to receive the honor. The following year, the port became the first on the U.S. West Coast to be awarded the U.S. Commerce Department's "E Star" Award for its efforts in encouraging and facilitating exports.

In 1981, China Ocean Shipping Company, one of the world's largest shipping companies, decided to inaugurate regular service between Asia and the U.S. West Coast and selected Long Beach as its first port of call.

The following year, the port opened its own Foreign Trade Zone and handled 824,900 containers. Twelve years later, that figure had jumped to more than 2.6 million.

In the 1980s, Southern California grew in importance as a revolving door for trade with the developing economies of Asia. That and the growth in the volume of containers moving between the region and inland U.S. points led the Port of Long Beach to partner with the Port of Los Angeles to jointly develop a $70-million, 150-acre Intermodal Container Transfer Facility, the first rail facility of its kind in the country.

Since 1994 alone, the port has undergone more than $1.35 billion in property purchases and capital projects to expand and upgrade its cargo-handling capabilities.

In 2007, the port handled 7.3 million containers—or more than 31 percent of all U.S. West Coast port container volumes—and more than 85 million metric tons of cargo, all valued at more than $140 billion. East Asian trade now accounts for more than 90 percent of the shipments through the port, with China, Japan, South Korea, Taiwan, Malaysia, and Singapore topping the list of its trading partners.

No longer an "option" to its San Pedro Bay neighbor, the Port of Long Beach stands on its own merit as an acknowledged leader in the utilization of cargo-handling technology and applying an intelligent approach toward making the port one of the most environmentally friendly in the world.

States Quartet, 1976. In a rare occurrence, four States Line freighters are seen tied up at Pier E. States Line suffered from strong foreign competition and the failure of its owners to make the shift to containerization in the 1970s. High fuel prices were blamed for the company's descent into bankruptcy in 1979. (Courtesy of the author's collection.)

ITS, 1976. The International Transportation Service (ITS) opened its 52-acre terminal on Pier J in 1972. The terminal was dredged to a depth of 42 feet to handle the most modern containerships and originally featured a 1,200-foot wharf and a pair of high-speed Paceco container cranes. (Courtesy of the author's collection.)

SOUTHEAST BASIN, 1978. As container cargo increasingly grew to dominate the port's business, Pier J (left) and Pier G (right) became the heart of cargo-handling activity at the Port of Long Beach. Pier J was originally developed in 1961 by the Connolly-Pacific Company and served as the heart of the port's container-handling operations. (Courtesy of the author's collection.)

PIER F, 1978. Four ships being worked at the break-bulk terminals on Pier F, while two Sea-Land Service and "K" Line containerships in the background are berthed at Piers G and J. A variety of bulk commodities await loading and unloading, including salt, coal, and steel. (Courtesy of the Port of Long Beach Archive.)

LYKES LINES, 1979. In the late 1970s, the New Orleans–based company operated a pair of roll-on/roll-off ships in the transpacific trades. The ships, the *Charles Lykes* and the *Tyson Lykes* seen docked at Pier D at the port, could hold a variety of wheeled vehicles, from tractors and school buses to ambulances and dump trucks, belowdecks as well as in containers on deck. (Courtesy of the author's collection.)

SEA-LAND SERVICE, 1979. The *Sea-Land Defender* was the first of Sea-Land's new D-9 class of container carriers and the first newly constructed diesel-powered containership to fly the U.S. flag. In 1971, Sea-Land Service moved its operations into a 95-acre container and rail/truck facility on Pier G. (Courtesy of the author's collection.)

HEAVY LIFT, 1979. The port's cargo-handling capability and its key location on the world's busiest trade routes have made for some interesting heavy-lift cargoes moving across its docks. This Japan-bound "Astro-Liner" was a highly popular, trailer-mounted carnival ride that used rear-projected film technology and high-tech special effects to simulate intergalactic space flight. (Courtesy of the Port of Long Beach Archive.)

SALEN SHIPPING, 1980. Sweden's Salen Shipping Company has specialized in the ocean transport of refrigerated cargoes since the 1930s. At the time, the company was the largest operator of reefer ships in the world. The company's white-hulled ships moved countless shipments of citrus fruit through its facility on Pier E. (Courtesy of the Port of Long Beach Archive.)

PRESIDENTIAL VISIT, 1982. The fully loaded containership *Sea-Land Explorer* provided the backdrop as Pres. Ronald Reagan signed the Export Trading Company Act of 1982 into law at the Sea-Land container terminal at Berth 228 on Pier G. (Courtesy of the Port of Long Beach Archive.)

QUEEN MARY AND DOME, 1983. The *Queen Mary* is seen here at her final berth on Pier J. The adjacent geodesic dome—the largest structure of its kind in the world—was specifically designed by Buckminster Fuller's longtime associate, Don Richter, to house the HK-1 "Spruce Goose" flying boat. (Courtesy of the author's collection.)

UNDER COVER, 1983. The massive HK-1 rests inside the geodesic dome built to protect it from the elements. The legendary flying boat would remain in the dome until it was acquired, disassembled, and moved by barge to the Evergreen Aviation Museum in McMinnville, Oregon, in 1992. (Courtesy of the Port of Long Beach Archive.)

THE *EAGLE* ARRIVES, 1984. Hundreds of sailboats escort the U.S. Coast Guard training bark *Eagle* as she glides into the port for the celebration of OPSail '84. The event gathered more than 20 square-rigged sailing ships from all over the world and was held in conjunction with the 1984 Olympic Games in Los Angeles. (Courtesy of the Port of Long Beach Archive.)

AUTOS BY SEA, 1986. Ships specifically designed to carry autos became frequent visitors to the Port of Long Beach as the volume of motor vehicles increased year by year. Honda's *World Wing II* was one of several ships the Japanese company used to carry autos and other vehicles to the port. (Courtesy of the Port of Long Beach Archive.)

ICTF, 1986. The 250-acre Intermodal Container Transfer Facility (ICTF) is a near-dock rail yard located approximately 5 miles from the ports of Long Beach and Los Angeles. The $55-million rail yard is a multiuser facility serving numerous shipping lines and is operated by the Union Pacific Railroad. (Courtesy of the Port of Long Beach Archive.)

PACIFIC TOWBOAT, 1988. A subsidiary of Foss Maritime, Pacific Towboat and Salvage Company has offered towing and tugboat service at the port since 1987. The 5,000-horsepower, diesel-powered *Pacific Escort* was one of the company's most powerful tractor tugs and can be seen here preparing to ease the auto carrier *Century Leader No. 5* away from her berth. (Courtesy of the author's collection.)

OIL ON PIER B, 1989. The tanker *Texaco Massachusetts* unloads a cargo of crude oil at the petroleum terminal on Pier B. Twenty-three years before, the ship was involved in a collision with a British tanker off New York that took the lives of 33 men. (Courtesy of the author's collection.)

LUMBER IMPORTS, 1989. Cut lumber was the first cargo unloaded at the Port of Long Beach and, over the years, has remained a major commodity handled at several of its terminals. The break-bulker *Newton* has cleared the breakwater with an inbound deckload of cut lumber from British Columbia. (Courtesy of the author's collection.)

COOL CARRIERS, 1989. Successor to Sweden's Salen Shipping, Cool Carriers operates a variety of refrigerated ships that call at the port with a variety of temperature-sensitive cargoes from all over the world. The company's fleet was comprised of ships flying the flag of several countries, including the *Racisce*, which sailed under the Yugoslav and later the Croatian flags. (Courtesy of the author's collection.)

FRUIT IMPORTS, 1990. The vast amount of fruits and vegetables grown in the United States during the summer months—particularly citrus fruit from California—is both consumed in the United States and exported to markets all over the world. During the rest of the year, much of the fruit and vegetables purchased in U.S. supermarkets throughout the United States are imported from other countries. Every year, thousands of crates of tamarillos, apples, and apricots are shipped in from New Zealand, while winter asparagus arrives from Peru, and grapes and stone fruit such as peaches are imported from Chile. Over the years, the Port of Long Beach has been a primary port of call for a number of steamship companies serving this highly specialized trade. Two Scandinavian companies—Sweden's Salen Shipping and J. Lauritzen of Denmark—dominated the refrigerated-cargo trade at the port for many years. (Courtesy of the author's collection.)

NAVY YARD, 1991. Two World War II–era combat veterans, the battleships USS *Missouri* (BB-62, foreground) and USS *New Jersey* (BB-63) were returned to active duty and modernized at the Long Beach Navy Yard in the late 1980s. The ships returned to the facility in 1991 to be decommissioned for the last time. The frigate USS *Ford* (FFG-54) and an unidentified destroyer are berthed in the background. (Courtesy of the author's collection.)

BARGE WORK, 1992. As in earlier days, the work to maintain the breakwater and bulkheads that protect the Port of Long Beach from the elements is a never-ending task. A barge-mounted Connolly-Pacific crane and a load of rock await the start of the next project. (Courtesy of the Port of Long Beach Archive.)

HANJIN SHIPPING COMPANY, 1995. Hanjin Shipping is Korea's largest carrier, with a fleet of more than 200 ships moving more than 100 million tons of cargo annually on 60 global routes linking 70 ports around the world. The company was founded after the end of World War II, inaugurated its first container service in 1969 in cooperation with Sea-Land service, and began calling at the Port of Long Beach in 1992. The company currently operates the largest container terminal at the port, the 385-acre TTI Terminal. The container facility is dredged to a depth of 55 feet and features 14 gantry cranes serving 5,000 feet of berth space. On-dock rail capability gives the terminal the capacity to handle four container trains at once. The $575-million terminal opened for business in 2002. Two years later, Hanjin became the first Korean carrier to place an order of five 10,000 TEU containerships, scheduled for deployment in the transpacific trades starting in 2010. (Courtesy of the author's collection.)

"K" LINE, 1994. Wearing the distinctive red funnel and white "K" of the Kawasaki Kaisen Kaisha, the containership *Brooklyn Bridge* departs the port for the Far East. "K" Line began operations in 1919 and has made Long Beach a regular port of call on its primary transpacific route since the early 1950s. In 2006 alone, "K" Line vessels made 345 callings at port. (Courtesy of the author's collection.)

LAST PILE, 1996. Exactly 2,388 concrete piles, each weighing several tons, were driven into the harbor floor to provide the foundation for the new Hanjin container terminal on Pier A. Port officials, engineers, and workers from contractor Manson Construction gather to celebrate the placement of the last pile. (Courtesy of the Port of Long Beach Archive.)

SPACE SERVICES, 1996. Sea Launch LLP is an international partnership of American, Russian, Ukrainian, and Norwegian aerospace companies providing geosynchronous heavy-lift launch services for commercial satellite customers. As of March 2008, it had assembled and launched 26 rockets carrying communications satellites for customers such as EchoStar, DirecTV, XM Satellite Radio, and PanAmSat. Sea Launch has a reciprocal agreement with France's Arianespace, providing mutual assistance in case either company's system is not able to launch a payload. This was used for the first time in 2004 when Arianespace's Ariane 5 had to reschedule a group of launches for reliability reasons. Managed by Boeing, the company's command ship and launch platform (below) are homeported at the Port of Long Beach. (Both, courtesy of Sea Launch LLP.)

Coke for Export, 1997. The Liberian-flag bulker *China Prosperity* takes on a load of coke at the Metropolitan Stevedore Company bulk facility on Pier G. In 1997, the port moved more than 19.5 million tons of bulk commodities such as coal, animal feeds, salt, and fertilizer. (Courtesy of the author's collection.)

New Cranes, 1997. In July, the *Dock Express 10* delivered the last two of a series of six 1,100-ton container cranes to the new Hanjin terminal on Pier T. The cranes were built by the Mitsui Engineering and Shipbuilding Company. The limited 155-foot clearance under the Gerald Desmond Bridge meant the cranes had to be transported only partly erect, with the fully assembled top sections temporarily secured between the legs. (Courtesy of the Port of Long Beach Archive.)

CHINA SHIPPING, 1998. The China Ocean Shipping Company, also known as COSCO, is China's largest ocean carrier. The company was founded in 1961 and has made the Port of Long Beach its Southern California port of call since the 1980s. The company currently offers weekly service linking the port with distribution centers in Asia. (Courtesy of the author's collection.)

HYUNDAI MERCHANT MARINE, 2001. Founded in 1976, Korea-based Hyundai Merchant Marine has grown to be one of the major carriers servicing the transpacific trade lanes. The company's fleet is made up of more than 119 ships, including full container carriers, LMG (Liquefied Methane Gas) carriers, oil tankers, bulk, and other carriers. (Courtesy of the Port of Long Beach Archive.)

CHINA SERVICE, 2004. The newly built, $107-million containership MV *Manukai* and a sister ship, the MV *Manuwili*, were put into service by the Matson Navigation Company on a biweekly service linking Long Beach with ports in China via Hawaii and Guam. The diesel-powered, 2,600-TEU ship was the first new build for Matson. (Courtesy of the Matson Navigation Company.)

CHANNEL BRIDGE, 2004. The 410-foot-long suspended main span was completed in 1968 and connects Terminal Island on its east side to downtown Long Beach. A study is under way to replace it with a long-span, cable-stayed bridge, a joint-venture project that could cost $800 million and be completed by 2016. (Courtesy of the Port of Long Beach Archive.)

PIER T, 2006. The Pier T container facility at Berths 132–140 serves eight container lines, including Hanjin, COSCO, China Shipping, "K" Line, and Yang Ming Line. The facility covers more than 385 acres with 5,000 feet of berthing space, 14 gantry cranes, and an on-dock rail with a capacity for four double-stack trains. (Courtesy of the Port of Long Beach Archive.)

SECURITY DRILL, 2006. The terrorist attacks of 9/11 spurred an unprecedented effort to secure the nation's ports from assaults that could literally paralyze the U.S. economy. Here a U.S. Coast Guard HH-60 Seahawk helicopter inserts an armed USCG assault team in a security drill held at the Port of Long Beach. (Courtesy of the Port of Long Beach Archive.)

A ROYAL SALUTE, 2006. In a truly historic meeting, the new Cunard liner *Queen Mary 2* sailed into the Port of Long Beach on February 23 after visiting several ports in South America. Escorted by a flotilla of smaller craft, the ship met her namesake, the original RMS *Queen Mary*, and exchanged a "whistle salute," which was heard more than 10 miles away. (Courtesy of the Cunard Steamship Company.)

HIGH-LEVEL VISIT, 2007. The national and local media were on hand when secretary of homeland security Michael Chertoff and congresswoman Jane Harmon visited the port to oversee the first field tests of a new radiation-detection system designed to protect the port from potential nuclear terrorist threats. (Courtesy of the Port of Long Beach Archive.)

PORT PROGRESS, 2008. Two-way trade moving through the Port of Long Beach—the second-busiest container port in the United States and the 16th busiest in the world—directly and indirectly supports one in eight jobs, or about 33,000, in the city of Long Beach; more than 316,000 in Southern California; and about 1.4 million throughout the United States. Since 2005, the port's Green Port Policy has spurred several programs, including the "Green Leases" project to create partnerships with terminal operators to improve air quality, the "Green Flag Vessel Speed Reduction Program" to reduce air pollution by more than 400 tons a year, and its pursuit of new environmental technologies such as shore-side electrical power to reduce emissions from docked vessels. The port handled more than 87 million metric tons of general cargo and 7.3 million containers in 2007—the equivalent of 33 percent of all the cargo moving in and out of all California ports, 26 percent moving through all West Coast ports, and 13 percent handled at all U.S. ports. (Courtesy of the Port of Long Beach Archive.)

Bibliography

Benson, Howard M. *Steamships and Motorships of the West Coast.* Seattle, WA: Superior Publishing Company, 1968.

The Cunard White Star Quadruple-Screw Liner Queen Mary. New York, NY: Bonanza Books, 1979.

Case, Walter H. *A History of Long Beach and Vicinity.* Chicago, IL: S. J. Clarke Publishing Company, 1927.

Erie, Steven P. *Globalizing L.A.* Palo Alto, CA: Stanford University Press, 2004.

Furita, R., and Y. Hirai. *A Short History of the Japanese Merchant Marine.* Tokyo, Japan: Tokyo News Service Limited, 1961.

Krieger, Michael. *Where Rails Meet the Sea.* New York, NY: Metro Books, 1998.

Newell, Gordon, and Joe Williamson. *Pacific Lumber Ships.* New York, NY: Bonanza Books, 1960.

Sawyer, L. A., and W. H. Mitchell. *The Liberty Ships.* New York, NY: Lloyd's of London Press, Inc., 1985.

Spalding, William Andrew. *History and Reminiscences: Los Angeles City and County.* Los Angeles, CA: J. R. Finnell and Sons Publishing Company, 1931.

Tate, E. Mowbray. *Transpacific Steam.* Cranbury, NJ: Cornwall Books, 1986.

INDEX